The Ultimate Guide to

Chick Flicks

The Ultimate Guide to

Chick

BROADWAY BOOKS   NEW YORK

Flicks

THE ROMANCE,
THE GLAMOUR,
THE TEARS,
AND MORE!

Kim Adelman

BROADWAY

Broadway Books titles may be purchased for business or promotional use or for special sales. For information, please write to: Special Markets Department, Random House, Inc., 1745 Broadway, New York, NY 10019.

PRINTED IN THE UNITED STATES OF AMERICA

BROADWAY BOOKS and its logo, a letter B bisected on the diagonal, are trademarks of Random House, Inc.

Visit our website at www.broadwaybooks.com

First edition published 2005

Book design by Mauna Eichner

Library of Congress Cataloging-in-Publication Data
Adelman, Kim, 1964–
   The ultimate guide to chick flicks : the romance, the glamour, the tears, and more / Kim Adelman.
      p. cm.
   1. Motion pictures for women. 2. Motion pictures and women. I. Title.
PN1995.9.W6A33 2005
791 43'082—dc22
                                        2004054480

ISBN 0-7679-1818-5

10 9 8 7 6 5 4

Contents